Index for Quilts

Master Instructions for the 10-Minute Block Method, Sewing, Cutting and Binding are on Pages 10 - 15

Starburst
photo on pages 4 - 5
instructions on pages 16 - 17

Solar Winds
photo on pages 6 - 7
instructions on pages 18 - 19

Oasis
photo on pages 8 - 9
instructions on page 20

Time Saving Techniques Allow You to Sew More Quilts!

Large Sampler Quilt
photo on pages 30 - 31
instructions on pages 21 - 27

Garden Delights
photo on pages 32 - 33
instructions on page 28

Pom Pom de Paris
photo on pages 34 - 35
instructions on page 29

Starburst

pieced by Betty Nowlin
quilted by Julie Lawson

*Like flowers turning their faces to greet the dawn, the starburst centers of this quilt
sparkle with the promise of a new, happy day. Brighten someone's outlook with the gift
of a quilt crafted from the heart. Starburst promises to be a treasured heirloom.*

instructions on page 16 - 17

Windmills of My Mind Tablecloth

pieced by Donna Arends Hansen

Presentation is everything! Invite your family and friends to dine at a table that sets the mood with cheerful color. Create an attractive background for your culinary offerings with a winning design that promises to get everyone talking.

instructions on page 19

Solar Winds

pieced by Donna Arends Hansen
quilted by Sue Needle

Sunshine dances across a forest of pinwheels, happily spinning in the summer breeze. Solar Winds fills your room with energy, color and light. Brighten your home with this whimsical beauty today. The 10-Minute block technique makes it easy.

instructions on pages 18 - 19

pieced by Betty Nowlin
quilted by Julie Lawson

*Simple elegance brings a relaxing oasis of comfort to your home in a quilt
that will complement traditional cottage decor and soften the spaces in any
modern dwelling. Create a masterpiece your family will treasure. Make it
today, love it tonight. The 10-Minute block technique makes it possible.*

instructions on page 20

Basic Instructions for '10-Minute' Blocks

Block Construction Diagrams

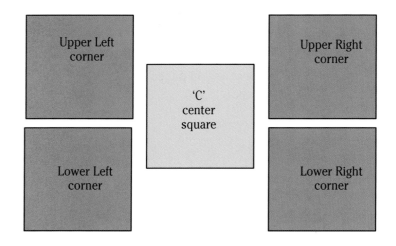

1. For each block you will need 4 corner squares and 1 'C' center square.

MAKING THE BLOCKS:
1. For each block, choose
    4 corner squares
    and
    1 center square.

REFER TO
    the Block Construction diagrams (illustration 1).

2. Fold a center square 'C' in half, wrong sides together. (illustration 2).

3. Align the raw edges of the folded square 'C' with the bottom and left edges of the upper right corner square. (illustration 3).

FOLLOW STEPS
    and illustrations 4 - 14 to complete the block.
    Repeat for more blocks.
    Each large block (that uses 10" x 10" squares) will measure $19\frac{1}{2}$" x $19\frac{1}{2}$" at this point.
    Each small block (that uses 5" x 5" squares) will measure $9\frac{1}{2}$" x $9\frac{1}{2}$" at this point.
    When 10" squares are used to make half-square triangle corner squares, the block will measure $18\frac{1}{2}$" x $18\frac{1}{2}$" at this point.

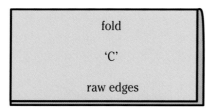

2. Fold the 'C' center square in half with wrong sides together.

'10-Minute' Blocks
10 Step Process

1. Choose the Block Set you like.
2. Choose the size of Quilt you want to make.
3. Cut all fabric strips, squares and pieces.
4. Assemble the large blocks.
5. Topstitch the edges of the center block.
6. Assemble the Quilt.
7. Add the borders.
8. Sandwich the backing, batting and top.
9. Stitch through all layers to make a quilt.
10. Finish the edges with binding.

**For a visual demonstration, visit
YouTube for a video titled '10-Minute Block Quilts'
by Suzanne McNeill**

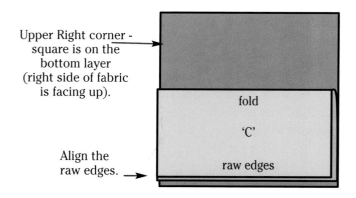

Upper Right corner - square is on the bottom layer (right side of fabric is facing up).

Align the raw edges.

3. Align the raw edges of the 'C' folded square with the bottom and left edges of the Upper Right corner square.

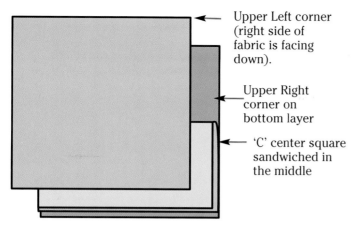

Upper Left corner (right side of fabric is facing down).

Upper Right corner on bottom layer

'C' center square sandwiched in the middle

4. Sandwich the 'C' folded square between the right sides of 2 corner squares so the right sides are touching 'C'.

There should be 4 layers of fabric along the bottom.

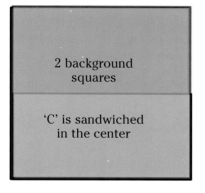

2 background squares

'C' is sandwiched in the center

5. Align the 4 layers of fabric along the bottom.

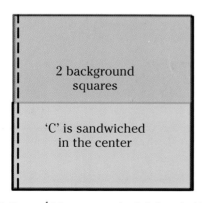

2 background squares

'C' is sandwiched in the center

6. Sew a $1/4$" seam on the left-hand side.

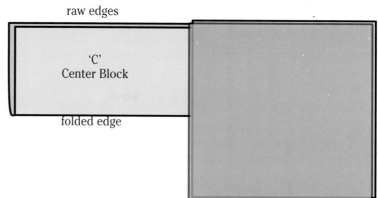

raw edges

'C' Center Block

folded edge

7. Open the layers so the Corner squares meet with wrong sides together.

Turn the piece to match the diagram.

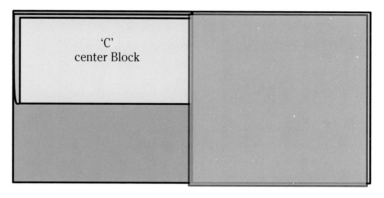

'C' center Block

8. Place the Lower Right corner square under 'C' folded square (right side of fabric facing up).

Align the top and left raw edges.

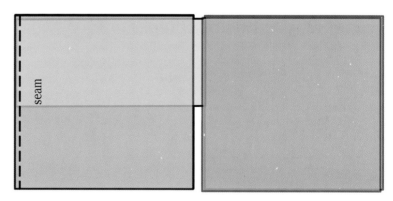

seam

9. Place the Lower Left corner square on top (right side of fabric facing down).

This layers the 'C' folded square between the right sides of the corner squares.

Align the left and top edges.

Sew a $1/4$" seam on the left side.

continued on the next page

continued from the previous page

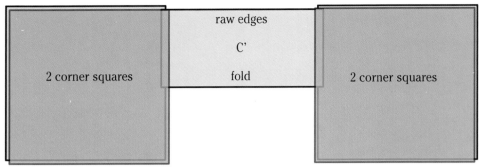

10. Open the corner squares with
wrong sides together. Press.

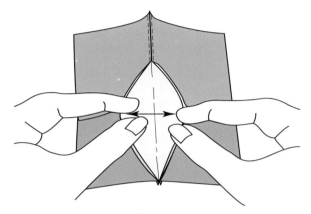

11. Pull the 'C' center square apart.

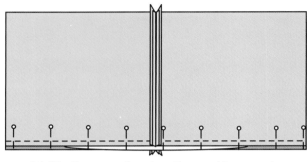

14. Pin the raw edges together making sure to
line up the seams in the center.

15. Sew a $1/4$" seam along the bottom edge.

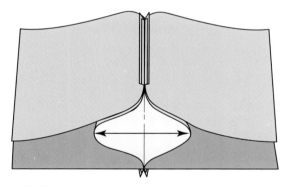

12. Flatten the seams with right sides together.
(opening up the 'C' center square
so it makes a diamond)

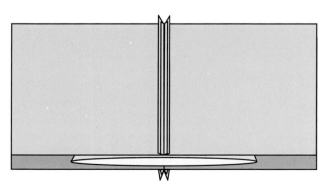

13. Pull the center shape until the shape is flat. Press.

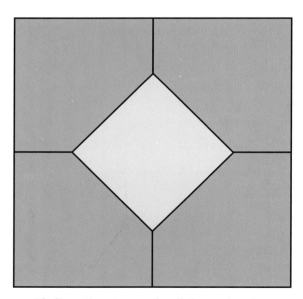

16. Open the piece and pull the center shape
until it is flat and the
'C' center forms a layered diamond. Press.

17. Choose Option 1 or Option 2 on page 13.
Topstitch the folded edge.

Terrific Tips:

At this point you have options:

1. Topstitch along edges of center square with decorative thread.

2. Gently pull the edge toward the center of the block forming a curve like a 'Cathedral Window' design. Topstitch or Blind Hem stitch the curves in place.

3. Embroider a design or save this space for a decorative quilting motif.

Option 1:
Quilt with Square Blocks in the Center

Option 1: 10-Minute Blocks Quilt with Square Blocks in the Center
Quilt Assembly Diagram

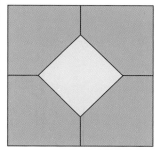

Square Blocks in the
Center
Make 6

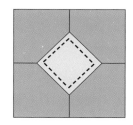

Topstitch along the
edges of each block
to hold the edges
down flat.

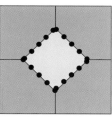

Or Topstitch along
the edges of each
block with a deco-
rative stitch

ASSEMBLY:
Arrange all blocks on a work surface or table.
Refer to diagram for block placement.
Sew blocks together in 3 rows, 2 blocks per row. Press.
Sew the rows together. Press.

Option 2:
Quilt with Curved Blocks in the Center

Cathedral Window

Create interesting 'Cathedral Window' style curves in the center of each large block. This technique is simple and creates a wonderfully mysterious look.

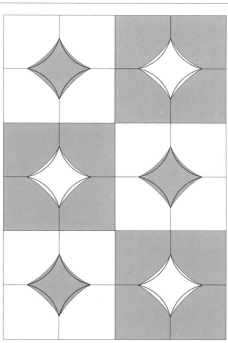

Option 2: 10-Minute Blocks Quilt with Curved Blocks in the Center
Quilt Assembly Diagram

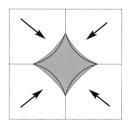

Gently pull the loose
edge of each side of
the center square
toward the center of
the block forming a
curve.

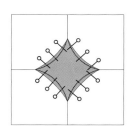

Pin in place.
Topstitch along the
INSIDE edges of
each center block
to hold the edges
down flat.

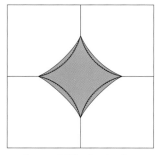

Curved Blocks in the
Center

ASSEMBLY:
Arrange all blocks on a work surface or table.
Refer to diagram for block placement.
Sew blocks together in 3 rows, 2 blocks per row. Press.
Sew the rows together. Press.

Rotary Cutting

Rotary Cutter: Friend or Foe

A rotary cutter is wonderful and useful. When not used correctly, the sharp blade can be a dangerous tool.
Follow these safety tips:

1. Never cut toward you.

2. Use a sharp blade. Pressing harder on a dull blade can cause the blade to jump the ruler and injure your fingers.

3. Always disengage the blade before the cutter leaves your hand, even if you intend to pick it up immediately.

Rotary cutters have been caught when lifting fabric, have fallen onto the floor and have cut fingers.

Basic Sewing

You now have precisely cut strips that are exactly the correct width. You are well on your way to blocks that fit together perfectly. Accurate sewing is the next important step.

Matching Edges:

1. Carefully line up the edges of your strips. Many times, if the underside is off a little, your seam will be off by $\frac{1}{8}$". This does not sound like much until you have 8 seams in a block, each off by $\frac{1}{8}$". Now your finished block is a whole inch wrong!

2. Pin the pieces together to prevent them shifting.

Seam Allowance:

I cannot stress enough the importance of accurate $\frac{1}{4}$" seams. All the quilts in this book are measured for $\frac{1}{4}$" seams unless otherwise indicated.

Most sewing machine manufacturers offer a Quarter-inch foot. A Quarter-inch foot is the most worthwhile investment you can make in your quilting.

Pressing:

I want to talk about pressing even before we get to sewing because proper pressing can make the difference between a quilt that wins a ribbon at the quilt show and one that does not.

Press, do NOT iron. What does that mean? Many of us want to move the iron back and forth along the seam. This "ironing" stretches the strip out of shape and creates errors that accumulate as the quilt is constructed. Believe it or not, there is a correct way to press your seams, and here it is:

1. Do NOT use steam with your iron. If you need a little water, spritz it on.

2. Place your fabric flat on the ironing board without opening the seam. Set a hot iron on the seam and count to 3. Lift the iron and move to the next position along the seam. Repeat until the entire seam is pressed. This sets and sinks the threads into the fabric.

3. Now, carefully lift the top strip and fold it away from you so the seam is on one side. Usually the seam is pressed toward the darker fabric, but often the direction of the seam is determined by the piecing requirements.

4. Press the seam open with your fingers. Add a little water or spray starch if it wants to close again. Lift the iron and place it on the seam. Count to 3. Lift the iron again and continue until the seam is pressed. Do NOT use the tip of the iron to push the seam open. So many people do this and wonder later why their blocks are not fitting together.

5. Most critical of all: For accuracy every seam must be pressed before the next seam is sewn.

Working with 'Crosswise Grain' Strips:

Strips cut on the crosswise grain (from selvage to selvage) have problems similar to bias edges and are prone to stretching. To reduce stretching and make your quilt lay flat for quilting, keep these tips in mind.

1. Take care not to stretch the strips as you sew.

2. Adjust the sewing thread tension and the presser foot pressure if needed.

3. If you detect any puckering as you go, rip out the seam and sew it again. It is much easier to take out a seam now than to do it after the block is sewn.

Sewing Bias Edges:

Bias edges wiggle and stretch out of shape very easily. They are not recommended for beginners, but even a novice can accomplish bias edges if these techniques are employed.

1. Stabilize the bias edge with one of these methods:

   a) Press with spray starch.

   b) Press freezer paper or removable iron-on stabilizer to the back of the fabric.

   c) Sew a double row of stay stitches along the bias edge and $\frac{1}{8}$" from the bias edge. This is a favorite technique of garment makers.

2. Pin, pin, pin! I know many of us dislike pinning, but when working with bias edges, pinning makes the difference between intersections that match and those that do not.

Building Better Borders:

Wiggly borders make a quilt very difficult to finish. However, wiggly borders can be avoided with these techniques.

1. Cut the borders on grain. That means cutting your strips parallel to the selvage edge.

2. Accurately cut your borders to the exact measure of the quilt.

3. If your borders are piece stripped from crosswise grain fabrics, press well with spray starch and sew a double row of stay stitches along the outside edge to maintain the original shape and prevent stretching.

4. Pin the border to the quilt, taking care not to stretch the quilt top to make it fit. Pinning reduces slipping and stretching.

Basic Layering Instructions

Marking Your Quilt:
If you choose to mark your quilt for hand or machine quilting, it is much easier to do so before layering. Press your quilt before you begin. Here are some handy tips regarding marking.
1. A disappearing pen may vanish before you finish.
2. Use a White pencil on dark fabrics.
3. If using a washable Blue pen, remember that pressing may make the pen permanent.

Pieced Backings:
1. Press the backing fabric before measuring.
2. If possible cut backing fabrics on grain, parallel to the selvage edges.
3. Piece 3 parts rather than 2 whenever possible, sewing 2 side borders to the center. This reduces stress on the pieced seam.
4. Backing and batting should extend at least 2" on each side of the quilt.

Creating a Quilt Sandwich:
1. Press the backing and top to remove all wrinkles.
2. Lay the backing wrong side up on the table.
3. Position the batting over the backing and smooth out all wrinkles.
4. Center the quilt top over the batting leaving a 2" border all around.
5. Pin the layers together with 2" safety pins positioned a hand-width apart. A grapefruit spoon makes inserting the pins easier. Leaving the pins open in the container speeds up the basting on the next quilt.

Basic Mitered Binding

A Perfect Finish:
The binding endures the most stress on a quilt and is usually the first thing to wear out. For this reason, we recommend using a double fold binding.
1. Trim the backing and batting even with the quilt edge.
2. If possible cut strips on the crosswise grain because a little bias in the binding is a Good thing. This is the only place in the quilt where bias is helpful, for it allows the binding to give as it is turned to the back and sewn in place.
3. Strips are usually cut 2½" wide, but check the instructions for your project before cutting.
4. Sew strips end to end to make a long strip sufficient to go all around the quilt plus 4"- 6".
5. With wrong sides together, fold the strip in half lengthwise. Press.
6. Stretch out your hand and place your little finger at the corner of the quilt top. Place the binding where your thumb touches the edge of the quilt. Aligning the edge of the quilt with the raw edges of the binding, pin the binding in place along the first side.
7. Leaving a 2" tail for later use, begin sewing the binding to the quilt with a ¼" seam.

For Mitered Corners:
1. Stop ¼" from the first corner. Leave the needle in the quilt and turn it 90°. Hit the reverse button on your machine and back off the quilt leaving the threads connected.
2. Fold the binding perpendicular to the side you sewed, making a 45° angle. Carefully maintaining the first fold, bring the binding back along the edge to be sewn.
3. Carefully align the edges of the binding with the quilt edge and sew as you did the first side. Repeat this process until you reach the tail left at the beginning. Fold the tail out of the way and sew until you are ¼" from the beginning stitches.
4. Remove the quilt from the machine. Fold the quilt out of the way and match the binding tails together. Carefully sew the binding tails with a ¼" seam. You can do this by hand if you prefer.

Finishing the Binding:
5. Trim the seam to reduce bulk.
6. Finish stitching the binding to the quilt across the join you just sewed.
7. Turn the binding to the back of the quilt. To reduce bulk at the corners, fold the miter in the opposite direction from which it was folded on the front.
8. Hand-sew a Blind stitch on the back of the quilt to secure the binding in place.

Basic Quilting Instructions

Hand Quilting:
Many quilters enjoy the serenity of hand quilting. Because the quilt is handled a great deal, it is important to securely baste the sandwich together. Place the quilt in a hoop and don't forget to hide your knots.

Machine Quilting:
All the quilts in this book were machine quilted. Some were quilted on a large, free-arm quilting machine and others were quilted on a sewing machine. If you have never machine quilted before, practice on some scraps first.

Straight Line Machine Quilting Tips:
1. Pin baste the layers securely.
2. Set up your sewing machine with a size 80 quilting needle and a walking foot.
3. Experimenting with the decorative stitches on your machine adds interest to your quilt. You do not have to quilt the entire piece with the same stitch. Variety is the spice of life, so have fun trying out stitches you have never used before as well as your favorite stand-bys.

Free Motion Machine Quilting Tips:
1. Pin baste the layers securely.
2. Set up your sewing machine with a spring needle, a quilting foot, and lower the feed dogs.

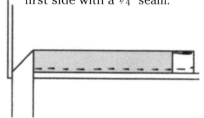

Align the raw edge of the binding with the raw edge of the quilt top. Start about 8" from the corner and go along the first side with a ¼" seam.

Stop ¼" from the edge. Then stitch a slant to the corner (through both layers of binding)... lift up, then down, as you line up the edge. Fold the binding back.

Align the raw edge again. Continue stitching the next side with a ¼" seam as you sew the binding in place.

Starburst

photos are on pages 4 - 5

FINISHED SIZE: 56" x 77"

YARDAGE:
We used Moda's 'Sunkissed' collection by Sweetwater
   or use the fabric colors of your choice.
   We purchased: 1 Layer Cake collection of 10" squares.

You will need the following squares (from the collection) OR yardage:
24 squares	OR $1\frac{3}{4}$ yards of assorted Light prints
Star Points, Border #1	Purchase $\frac{7}{8}$ yard Medium (Gold)
Centers & Sashing	Purchase $1\frac{1}{8}$ yards of Dark print (Green)
Border #2 & Binding	Purchase 2 yards of Light/Medium print
Backing	Purchase $4\frac{1}{4}$ yards
Batting	Purchase 64" x 85"

Sewing machine, needle, thread

1. BACKGROUND SQUARES:
   Cut 24 Light squares, each 10" x 10".

Make Perfect Star Points

2. MAKE THE STAR POINTS:
   Cut 24 Gold rectangles, each $4\frac{1}{2}$" x $6\frac{1}{2}$".
   Follow the steps to Make Perfect Points to form 24 triangles.

  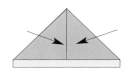

a. Fold a $\frac{1}{4}$" hem on one long side of each rectangle. Press the hem to make a finished edge.

b. Fold the piece in half and press to mark the center line. Fold the corner to meet the center line. It will not meet at the bottom. Press.

c. Fold the other corner to meet the center line. It will line up with the first corner but will not line up with the bottom. Press.

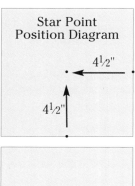

Star Point Position Diagram

4½"

4½"

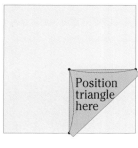

Position triangle here

3. POSITION THE STAR POINTS:
   Refer to the diagram.
   Measure $4\frac{1}{2}$" from each edge of the background squares. Lightly mark 3 dots as shown with a wash-away pen or pencil.
   Position the corner and short sides of the Gold triangle with the dots as shown. Position the triangle with the folded side down and pin securely.
   Refer to Option 2 on page 13. Roll the bias edge in the shape of a curve and topstitch as in Option 2.
   Trim away the dog-ears along the edge of the block.

4. CUT THE 'C' CENTER SQUARES:
   Cut 6 Dark print squares, each 12" x 12".

5. SORT FOR EACH BLOCK:
   Choose 4 squares with a Star Point for each block background.
   Match a Dark center square with each set of 4 squares.

6. 10-MINUTE BLOCKS:
   Sew 6 blocks with a Green center following the 10-Minute method on pages 10 - 13.
   Refer to the Option 2 section of the 10-Minute Block instructions on page 13. Roll the bias edge in the shape of a curve and topstitch as in Option 2.

Block Construction Diagrams

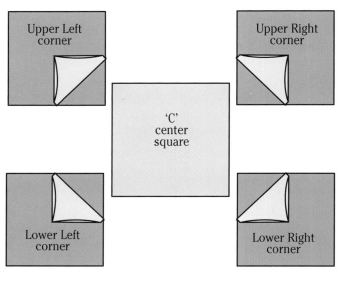

1. For each block you will need 4 squares (with a triangle stitched onto each as in the diagram) and 1 'C' center square.

Follow steps and illustrations 2 - 9 on pages 10 - 13.

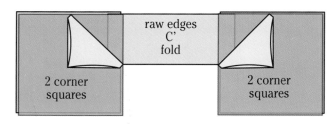

10. Open the corner squares with wrong sides together. Press.

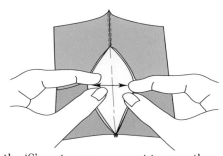

11. Pull the 'C' center square apart to open the pocket.

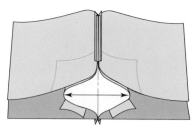

12. Flatten the seams with right sides together. (opening up the 'C' center square so it makes a diamond).

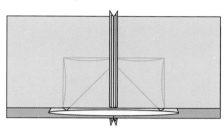

13. Pull the center shape until the shape is flat. Press

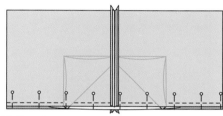

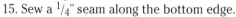

14. Pin the raw edges together making sure to line up the seams in the center.
15. Sew a $1/4$" seam along the bottom edge.

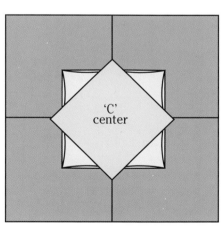

16. Open the piece and pull the center shape until it is flat and the 'C' center forms a layered diamond. Press.

17. Refer to Option 2 on page 13. Pin the bias edges back into a curve and topstitch in place.

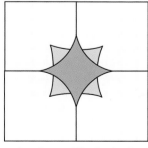

Starburst Block - Make 6

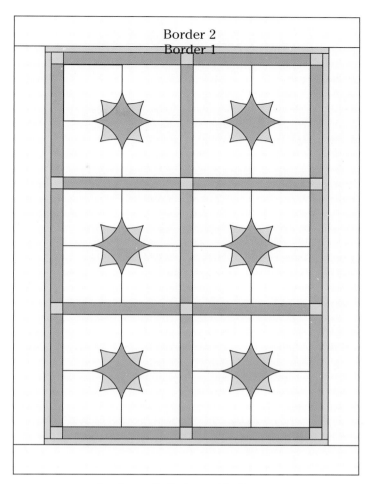

Starburst Quilt Assembly Diagram

7. SASHINGS & CORNERSTONES:
Cut 17 Dark (Green) sashing strips, each $2^1/2$" x $19^1/2$".
Cut 12 Medium (Gold) cornerstones, each $2^1/2$" x $2^1/2$".

8. ASSEMBLY:
Arrange blocks, sashing and cornerstones on a work surface.
Rows 1, 3, 5 & 7:
Sew a cornerstone-sash-cornerstone-sash-cornerstone. Press.
Rows 2, 4 & 6:
Sew a sash-block-sash-block-sash. Press.
Sew the rows together. Press.

9. BORDER #1:
Cut seven $1^1/2$" strips across the width of fabric and sew together end to end.
Cut 2 strips, each $1^1/2$" x $65^1/2$" for sides.
Cut 2 strips, each $1^1/2$" x $46^1/2$" for the top and bottom.
Sew side borders to the quilt. Press.
Sew top and bottom borders to the quilt. Press.

10. BORDER #2:
Cut strips $5^1/2$" wide parallel to the selvage to eliminate piecing.
Cut 2 strips, each $5^1/2$" x $67^1/2$" for sides.
Cut 2 strips, each $5^1/2$" x $56^1/2$" for top and bottom.
Sew side borders to the quilt. Press.
Sew top and bottom borders to the quilt. Press.

11. FINISHING:
Quilting: See Basic Instructions.
Binding: Cut strips $2^1/2$" wide.
Sew together end to end to equal 276".
See Binding Instructions.

Solar Winds

photos are on pages 6 - 7

FINISHED SIZE: 46" x 64"

YARDAGE:

We used Moda's 'Lovely' collection by Sandy Gervais
    or use the fabric colors of your choice.
    We purchased 1 Layer Cake collection of 10" squares.

You will need the following squares (from the collection) OR yardage:

6 squares	OR Purchase $\frac{5}{8}$ yard of Aqua print
6 squares	OR Purchase $\frac{5}{8}$ yard of Yellow print
6 squares	OR Purchase $\frac{5}{8}$ yard of Coral print
6 squares	OR Purchase $\frac{5}{8}$ yard of Ivory print
Centers	1 yard Aqua print
Border #1	Purchase $\frac{1}{4}$ yard of Aqua print
Border #2 & Binding	Purchase $1\frac{5}{8}$ yards of Ivory print
Backing	Purchase $2\frac{3}{4}$ yards
Batting	Purchase 54" x 72"

Sewing machine, needle, thread

1. IVORY/CORAL HALF-SQUARE TRIANGLES:
Cut 6 Ivory squares and 6 Coral squares, each 10" x 10".
Refer to the half-square triangle diagram to the right.
Sew 12 half-square triangles.

2. YELLOW/AQUA HALF-SQUARE TRIANGLES:
Cut 6 Yellow squares and 6 Aqua squares, each 10" x 10".
Refer to the half-square triangle diagram to the right.
Sew 12 half-square triangles.

3. CUT THE 'C' CENTERS:
Cut 6 squares of Aqua print, each 8" x 8".
    Note: If desired center a flower print in the square.

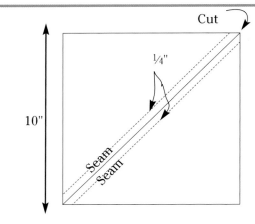

Half-Square Triangle Diagram

1. Place 2 squares right sides together.
2. Draw a diagonal line from corner to corner.
3. Stitch a SCANT $\frac{1}{4}$" on each side of the line.
4. Cut squares apart on the diagonal line.
5. Open the 2 new squares with 2 colors.
6. Press. Trim off dog-ears.
7. Center and trim to $9\frac{1}{2}$" x $9\frac{1}{2}$".

Light square   Dark square   Half-Square
Ivory or Yellow   Coral or Aqua   Triangle

4. 10-MINUTE BLOCKS:
Refer to the 10-Minute Block
    instructions on pages 10 - 13.

Block A:
Position 4 Ivory/Coral blocks in a pinwheel.
Sew the blocks together with a 10-Minute
    Block method, see pages 10 - 13.
Make 3 large blocks.

Block B:
Position 4 Yellow/Aqua blocks in a pinwheel.
Sew the blocks together with a 10-Minute
    Block method, see pages 10 - 13.
Make 3 large blocks.

Refer to the Option 2 section of the 10-Minute
    Block instructions on page 13. Roll the bias
    edge in the shape of a curve and
    topstitch as in Option 2.

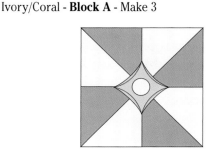

8" Fussy Cut Center

Upper Left corner   Upper Right corner

Coral / Ivory   Ivory / Coral

Coral / Ivory   Ivory / Coral

Lower Left corner   Lower Right corner

Ivory/Coral - **Block A** - Make 3

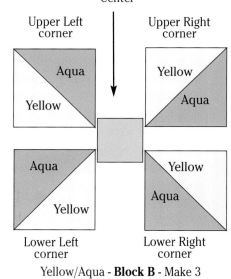

8" Fussy Cut Center

Upper Left corner   Upper Right corner

Aqua / Yellow   Yellow / Aqua

Aqua / Yellow   Yellow / Aqua

Lower Left corner   Lower Right corner

Yellow/Aqua - **Block B** - Make 3

Ivory/Coral
Block A
Make 3

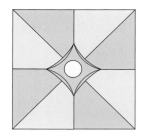

Yellow/Aqua
Block B
Make 3

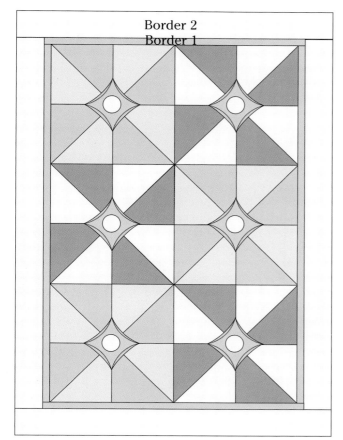

Border 2
Border 1

Solar Winds Quilt Assembly Diagram

5. ASSEMBLY:
Arrange the blocks on a work surface.
Sew 3 rows of 2 blocks each. Press.
Sew the rows together. Press.

6. BORDER #1:
Cut five $1\frac{1}{2}$" strips across the width of fabric and
sew together end to end.
Cut 2 strips $1\frac{1}{2}$" x $54\frac{1}{2}$" for sides.
Cut 2 strips $1\frac{1}{2}$" x $38\frac{1}{2}$" for the top and bottom.
Sew side borders to the quilt. Press.
Sew top and bottom borders to the quilt. Press.

7. BORDER #2:
Cut strips $4\frac{1}{2}$" wide parallel to the selvage to
eliminate piecing.
Cut 2 strips $4\frac{1}{2}$" x $56\frac{1}{2}$" for sides.
Cut 2 strips $4\frac{1}{2}$" x $46\frac{1}{2}$" for top and bottom.
Sew side borders to the quilt. Press.
Sew top and bottom borders to the quilt. Press.

8. FINISHING:
Quilting: See Basic Instructions.
Binding: Cut strips $2\frac{1}{2}$" wide.
Sew together end to end to equal 230".
See Binding Instructions.

Windmills of My Mind

photos are on pages 2 and 7
FINISHED SIZE: 40" x 58"
YARDAGE:
We used Moda's 'Lovely' collection by Sandy Gervais
or use the fabric colors of your choice.

Blocks	$\frac{7}{8}$ yard of Coral print
Blocks	$\frac{7}{8}$ yard of Ivory print
Centers	1 yard Aqua print
Border #1 & Binding	Purchase $\frac{5}{6}$ yard of Aqua print
Backing	Purchase $1\frac{2}{3}$ yards

Sewing machine, needle, thread

1. IVORY/CORAL HALF-SQUARE TRIANGLES:
Cut 12 Ivory squares and 12 Coral squares, each 10" x 10".
Refer to the half-square triangle diagram on page 18.
Sew 24 half-square triangles.

2. CUT THE 'C' CENTERS:
Cut 6 squares of Aqua print, each 8" x 8".
Note: If desired center a flower print in each square.

3. 10-MINUTE BLOCKS:
Position 4 Ivory-Coral blocks in a pinwheel (see illustration on
page 18, Block A.
Sew the blocks together with a 10-Minute Block method, see
pages 10 - 13. Make 6 large blocks.
Refer to the Option 2 section of the 10-Minute Block method
on page 13. Roll the bias edge in the shape of a curve and
topstitch as in Option 2.

4. ASSEMBLY:
Arrange the blocks on a work surface.
Sew 3 rows of 2 blocks each. Press.
Sew the rows together. Press.

5. BORDER #1:
Cut five $2\frac{1}{2}$"
strips across the
width of fabric
and sew together
end to end.
Cut 2 strips $2\frac{1}{2}$"
x $54\frac{1}{2}$" for sides.
Cut 2 strips $2\frac{1}{2}$"
x $40\frac{1}{2}$" for top and
bottom.
Sew side bor-
ders to quilt. Press.
Sew top and bot-
tom borders to the
quilt. Press.

6. BACKING:
Cut backing
fabric $40\frac{1}{2}$" x $58\frac{1}{2}$".

7. FINISHING:
Quilting: No batting
or quilting on the
tablecloth.
Binding: Cut strips
$2\frac{1}{2}$" wide. Sew
together end to end
to equal 206".
See Binding
Instructions.

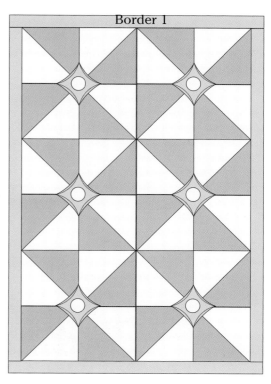

Border 1

Windmills of My Mind Assembly Diagram

Oasis

photos are on pages 8 - 9

FINISHED SIZE: 57" x 79"

YARDAGE:
We used Moda's 'Oasis' collection by 3 Sisters
    or use the fabric colors of your choice.

Background squares	Purchase ⅝ yard of Light print A
Background squares	Purchase ⅝ yard of Light print B
Background squares	Purchase ⅝ yard of Light print C
Background squares	Purchase ⅝ yard of Light print D
Centers, Border #1 & Sashing	Purchase 2 yards of Dark print
Border #2 & Binding	Purchase 2 yards of Light print E
Backing	Purchase 4⅓ yards
Batting	Purchase 65" x 87"
Sewing machine, needle, thread	

1. CUT THE 'C' CENTER SQUARES:
    TIP: Before you cut the 14" center squares, cut 3 strips
        $3\frac{1}{2}$" x $63\frac{1}{2}$" parallel to the selvage for the vertical sash
        and sides of Border #1 (see step 6).
    Cut the top/bottom Border #1 strips (see step 6) from
        the fabric.
    Cut 6 Dark squares, each 14" x 14" from the fabric.

2. CUT SQUARES FOR THE BLOCKS:
    From each Light print, cut six 10" x 10" squares
        for a total of 24 squares.
    Note: It will be easier to group the pieces (A-B-C-D) if you
        stack the fabrics and cut through 4 layers at once.

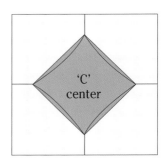

Oasis Block Diagram

3. 10-MINUTE BLOCKS:
    Match a Dark center with each group of 4 squares.

    Sew 6 blocks with a Dark center following the
        10-Minute method on pages 10 - 13.
    Refer to the Option 2 section of the 10-Minute
        Block instructions on page 13. Roll the bias edge
        in the shape of a curve and topstitch as in
        Option 2.

4. SASHING:
    Cut 4 Dark strips, each $3\frac{1}{2}$" x $19\frac{1}{2}$" for horizontal sashing.
    Use 1 Dark strip $3\frac{1}{2}$" x $63\frac{1}{2}$" for the middle vertical sashing.

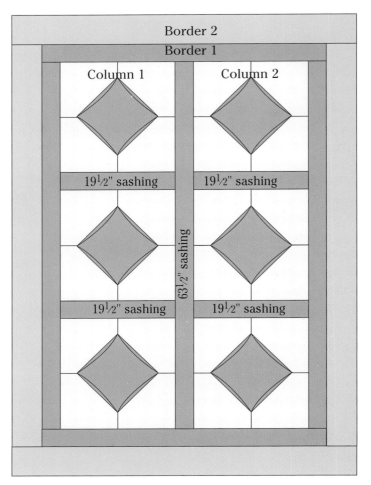

Oasis Quilt Assembly Diagram

5. ASSEMBLY:
    Arrange the blocks and sashing strips on a work surface.
    Column 1:
        Sew a block - $19\frac{1}{2}$" sashing - block - $19\frac{1}{2}$" sashing - block.
        Press.
    Repeat for Column 2.
    Sew the $63\frac{1}{2}$" middle sashing to the right side of Column 1.
        Press.
    Sew Column 2 to the Column 1 piece. Press.

6. BORDER #1:
Cut strips $3\frac{1}{2}$" wide parallel to the selvage to eliminate piecing.
    Cut 2 strips $3\frac{1}{2}$" x $63\frac{1}{2}$" for sides.
    Cut 2 strips $3\frac{1}{2}$" x $47\frac{1}{2}$" for top and bottom.
    Sew side borders to the quilt. Press.
    Sew top and bottom borders to the quilt. Press.

7. BORDER #2:
Cut strips $5\frac{1}{2}$" wide parallel to the selvage to eliminate piecing.
    Cut 2 strips $5\frac{1}{2}$" x $69\frac{1}{2}$" for sides.
    Cut 2 strips $5\frac{1}{2}$" x $57\frac{1}{2}$" for top and bottom.
    Sew side borders to the quilt. Press.
    Sew top and bottom borders to the quilt. Press.

8. FINISHING:
Quilting: See Basic Instructions.
Binding: Cut strips $2\frac{1}{2}$" wide.
        Sew together end to end to equal 282".
        See Binding Instructions.

FINISHED SIZE: 77" x 98"
YARDAGE:
We used Moda's 'Pom Pom de Paris' collection by French General
    or use the fabric colors of your choice.

Blocks	Purchase 3 yards Light print-A
Blocks	Purchase $3\frac{1}{2}$ yards Dark print-B
Blocks & Sashing	Purchase $1\frac{1}{2}$ yards Light print-C
Border #1 & Cornerstones	Purchase $\frac{1}{2}$ yards Dark print-D
Border #2 & Binding	Purchase $2\frac{1}{2}$ yards of Light print-E
Backing	Purchase 6 yards
Batting	Purchase 85" x 106"

Sewing machine, needle, thread

Large Sampler Quilt

photos are on pages 30 - 31
OPTIONAL SETTINGS
Sew the quilt together with 12 different blocks
as shown in the diagram on page 27
OR
Make 12 blocks from the SAME block pattern.
Note: These blocks are advanced projects.

BLOCK 1 - FOUR PATCH:

Cut 4 Dark print-B center 'C' squares, each 8" x 8".
Cut 16 Light print-A background squares, each $5\frac{1}{4}$" x $5\frac{1}{4}$".
Match a Dark print-B center with each group of 4 Light print-A squares.
Sew 4 blocks with a Dark center following the 10-Minute method on
    pages 10 - 13.
Refer to the Option 2 section of the 10-Minute Block on page 13. Roll
    the bias edge in the shape of a curve and topstitch as in Option 2.
Four Patch - Sew 4 blocks together. Press.

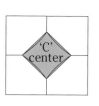

Make 4
10-Minute Blocks

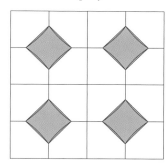

Four Patch

BLOCK 2 - FRAMED WINDOW

Cut 1 Light print-A center 'C' square 10" x 10".
Cut 4 Dark print-B background squares, each $8\frac{1}{4}$" x $8\frac{1}{4}$".
Cut 4 Light print-A side-1 border strips, each $2\frac{1}{4}$" x $8\frac{1}{4}$".
Cut 4 Light print-A side-2 strips, each $2\frac{1}{4}$" x 10".
Sew a side-1 border strip to one side of each Dark square.
    Press. Sew a side-2 strip to the next side of each
    Dark square. Press.
Framed Window - Sew 4 blocks with a Light print-A
    center following the 10-Minute method on pages 10 - 13.
Refer to the Option 2 section of the 10-Minute Block on
    page 13. Roll the bias edge in the shape of a curve
    and topstitch as in Option 2.

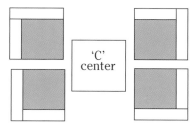

Make 4 dark squares,
each with two border strips.
Assemble a 10-Minute Block.

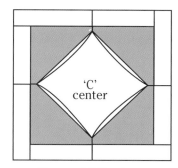

Framed Window

BLOCK 3 - HOURGLASS

Cut 4 Light print-A, each 10" x 10".
Cut 4 Dark print-B, each 10" x 10".
Corner Triangle Pieces:
Use 2 Dark print-B squares and 2 Light print-C squares.
Fold each square in half diagonally to make a triangle.
    Press.
Position a triangle on each background square as shown.
    Baste the triangles along the sides with a $\frac{1}{8}$" seam.
    Refer to the Option 2 section of the 10-Minute Block on
        page 13. Roll the bias edge in the shape of a curve
        and topstitch as in Option 2.
4-Square Center:
Cut 2 Light print-A and 2 Dark print-B squares, each $5\frac{1}{4}$" x $5\frac{1}{4}$".
Position the squares as shown.
Sew squares together to make a 10" x 10" square 'C'.
    Press. Position the center as shown.
Hourglass Block:
Sew 4 blocks with the 4-Square center following the
    10-Minute method on pages 10 - 13.
Refer to the Option 2 section of the 10-Minute Block on
    page 13. Roll the bias edge in the shape of a curve
    and topstitch as in Option 2.

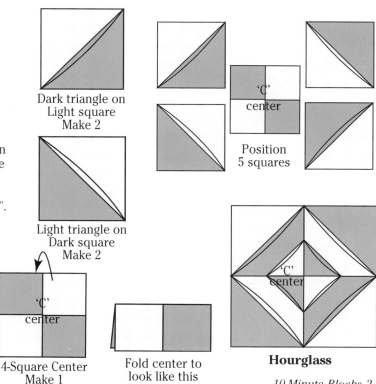

Dark triangle on
Light square
Make 2

Light triangle on
Dark square
Make 2

Position
5 squares

4-Square Center
Make 1

Fold center to
look like this

Hourglass

10-Minute Blocks 2 21

Light squares
10" x 10" - Cut 4

Dark squares
8" x 8"
Cut 4

Fold Dark
squares on
the diagonal
to form
triangles

Dark
rectangles
4½" x 6½"
Cut 4

Fold into
Star Point
triangles

Position a triangle
on each
background square
Make 4

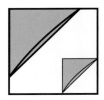

Position a Star Point
on the same
background square
Make 4

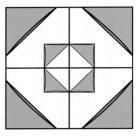

Position the 4 background blocks

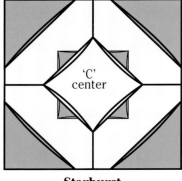

'C'
center

Starburst

BLOCK 4 - STARBURST

Cut 4 Light print-A squares for backgrounds, each 10" x 10".
Cut 1 Light print-C center 'C' square 12" x 12".

Triangles:

Cut 4 Dark print-B squares for corner triangles, each 8" x 8".
Fold each Dark square on the diagonal to form a triangle. Press.

Star Points:

Cut 4 Dark print-B rectangles for Star Points, each 4½" x 6½".
Fold each rectangle to make a Star Point triangle, see diagrams on page 16. Press.

Position Triangles and Star Points:

Position a triangle on each Light print-A background square.
Secure the edges of the triangles to the background squares with a ⅛" seam.
Position each Star Point on the same Light print-A background square, see page 16.
Topstitch in place and trim off the dog-ears.

Starburst Block:

Position the 4 background blocks in a square.
Sew the 4 background blocks with the Light print-C center 'C' square
following the 10-Minute method on pages 10 - 13.
Refer to the Option 2 section of the 10-Minute Block instructions on page 13.
Roll the bias edge in the shape of a curve and topstitch as in Option 2.

Light
squares
7" x 7"
Cut 8

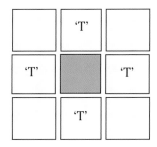

Position the 9 squares

Dark
squares
7" x 7"
Cut 5

Fold 4
Dark
squares
on the
diagonal
to form
triangles

Position a
triangle on
the 4 Light
'T' background
squares
Make 4

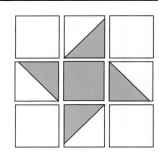

Sew squares together

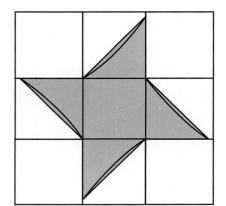

Friendship Star

BLOCK 5 - FRIENDSHIP STAR

Cut 8 Light print-A background squares, each 7" x 7".
Cut 5 Dark print-B squares, each 7" x 7".

Position Squares:

Position 9 squares (8 Light and 1 Dark) as shown.

Triangles:

Fold each of the remaining 4 Dark squares on the diagonal to form a triangle. Press.
Position a triangle on each of 4 Light 'T' background squares as shown.
Secure the edges of each triangle to the background square with a ⅛" seam.
Refer to the Option 2 section of the 10-Minute Block instructions on page 13.
Roll the bias edge in the shape of a curve and topstitch as in Option 2.

Friendship Star Block:

Sew the squares together as shown. Press.
Center the block and square it up to 19½" x 19½" by trimming ¼" from each side.

Light squares
10" x 10" - Cut 4

'C'
center

Dark square
16" x 16" - Cut 1

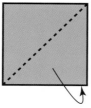

Dark squares
10" x 10"
Cut 4

Fold Dark
squares on the
diagonal to
form triangles

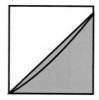

Position a triangle
on each square

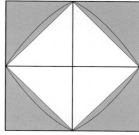

Position the 4
background blocks

BLOCK 6 - SPARKLE

Cut 4 Light print-A for background squares, each 10" x 10".
Cut 1 Dark print-B for center 'C' square 16" x 16".

Triangles:

Cut 4 Dark print-B squares for large triangles, each 10" x 10"
Fold each Dark square on the diagonal to form a triangle. Press.
Position a triangle on each Light background square as shown.
   Secure the edges of each triangle to the background square with a $1/8$" seam.
   Refer to the Option 2 section of the 10-Minute Block instructions on page
   13. Roll the bias edge in the shape of a curve and topstitch as in Option 2.

Sparkle Block:

Arrange the background squares as shown.
Sew the 4 background blocks with the Dark print-B center 'C' square
   following the10-Minute method on pages 10 - 13.
Refer to the Option 2 section of the 10-Minute Block instructions on page 13.
   Roll the bias edge in the shape of a curve and topstitch as in Option 2.

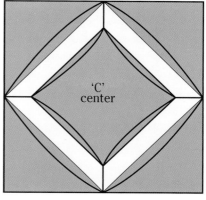

'C'
center

Sparkle

Dark square
10" x 10"
Cut 1

Light squares
$10\frac{1}{2}$" x $10\frac{1}{2}$"
Cut 2

Dark squares
$10\frac{1}{2}$" x $10\frac{1}{2}$"
Cut 2

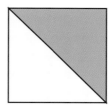

Light/Dark
Half-square
triangles
(see page 16)
Make 4

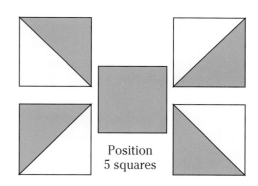

Position
5 squares

BLOCK 7 - WHIRLIGIG

Cut 1 Dark print-B for the center square 10" x 10".
Cut 2 Light print-A squares for half-square triangles, each $10\frac{1}{2}$" x $10\frac{1}{2}$".
Cut 2 Dark print-B squares for half-square triangles, each $10\frac{1}{2}$" x $10\frac{1}{2}$".

Half-Square Triangles:

Make 4 Light/Dark half-square triangles (see instructions on page 18).
Center and trim to 10" x 10".

Whirligig Block:

Arrange the background squares in a pinwheel.
Sew the 4 background blocks with the Dark print-B center 'C' square
   following the 10-Minute method on pages 10 - 13.
Refer to the Option 2 section of the 10-Minute Block instructions on page 13.
   Roll the bias edge in the shape of a curve and topstitch as in Option 2.

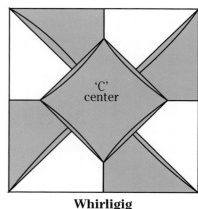

'C'
center

Whirligig

BLOCK 8 - ORANGE PEEL

Cut 16 Dark print-B background squares, each 5¼" x 5¼".
Cut 5 Light print-A center 'C' squares, each 7" x 7".

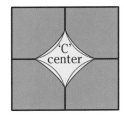

Make 4 Blocks

Make 10-Minute Blocks:

Match 4 Dark squares with 1 Light square.
Sew squares together following the 10-Minute method on pages 10 - 13.
Refer to the Option 2 section of the 10-Minute Block instructions on page 13. Roll the bias edge in the shape of a curve and topstitch as in Option 2.
Make 4.

Blocks with an Extra Center:

Follow the instructions below.

Blocks with an Extra Center

Note: Adding 'Extra Centers' is an advanced technique,

I suggest that beginners sew a simple block with 4 squares (see Four-Patch on page 21).

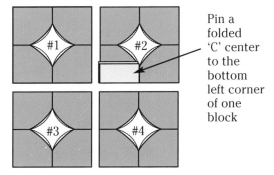

Pin a folded 'C' center to the bottom left corner of one block

ASSEMBLY

1. Arrange 4 blocks on a table.
2. Number the blocks #1, #2, #3, and #4.
3. Pin a 'C' folded center to the bottom left corner of block #2, aligning the left and bottom raw edges.

4. Place block #1 over block #2 with right sides together.
5. Sew along the left side. Press.

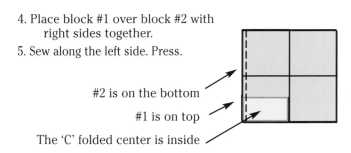

#2 is on the bottom

#1 is on top

The 'C' folded center is inside

Note: Block #1 is wrong side up.

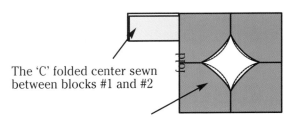

The 'C' folded center sewn between blocks #1 and #2

Note: #2 is folded under block #1.

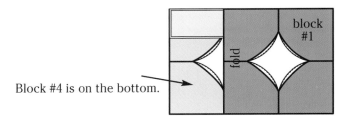

Block #4 is on the bottom.

6. Open the sewn blocks #1 & #2.
   Fold with wrong sides together and the folded 'C' center sticking out as shown.
7. Turn the piece to match the diagram.
8. Lay block #4 on a table with the right side up.
9. Align the 'C' folded center of #1/#2 with the upper left corner of block #4.

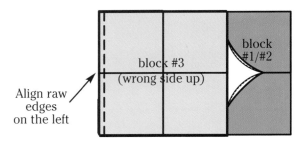

Align raw edges on the left

10. Place block #3 on top, right sides together, aligning the left raw edges.
11. Sew along the left side. Press.

Follow steps and illustrations 10 - 16 on pages 10 - 13.

Sew the blocks together as shown.
   Refer to the Option 2 section of the 10-Minute Block instructions on page 13. Roll the bias edge in the shape of a curve and topstitch as in Option 2.

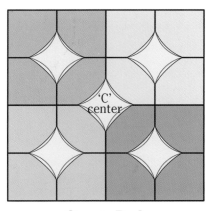

Orange Peel

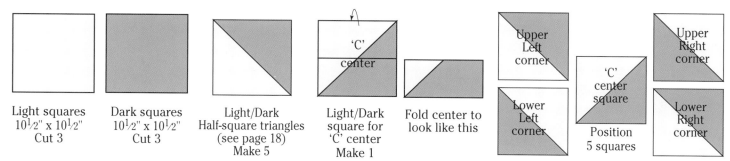

Light squares
10½" x 10½"
Cut 3

Dark squares
10½" x 10½"
Cut 3

Light/Dark
Half-square triangles
(see page 18)
Make 5

Light/Dark
square for
'C' center
Make 1

Fold center to
look like this

Upper Left corner

Lower Left corner

'C' center square

Position 5 squares

Upper Right corner

Lower Right corner

BLOCK 9 - SUNSHINE & SHADOWS

Half-Square Triangles:
    Cut 3 Light print-A squares for half-square triangles, each 10½" x 10½" .
    Cut 3 Dark print-B squares for half-square triangles, each 10½" x 10½" .
    Make 5 Light/Dark half-square triangles (see page 18). Center and trim each to 10" x 10".

'C' Center of Block:
    Fold the center half-square triangle as shown.

Sunshine and Shadows Block:
    Position 5 squares as shown. Pay careful attention to the placement of the 'C' center
        so the light and dark sections end up in the correct position.
    Sew the 4 background blocks with the Light/Dark center following the
        10-Minute method on pages 10 - 13.
    Refer to the Option 2 section of the 10-Minute Block instructions on page 13.
        Roll the bias edge in the shape of a curve and topstitch as in Option 2.

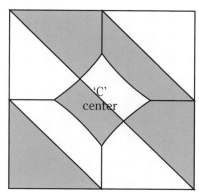

Sunshine & Shadows

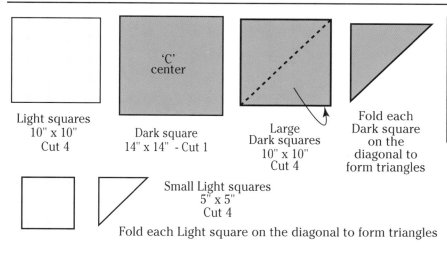

Light squares
10" x 10"
Cut 4

Dark square
'C' center
14" x 14" - Cut 1

Large
Dark squares
10" x 10"
Cut 4

Fold each
Dark square
on the
diagonal to
form triangles

Small Light squares
5" x 5"
Cut 4

Fold each Light square on the diagonal to form triangles

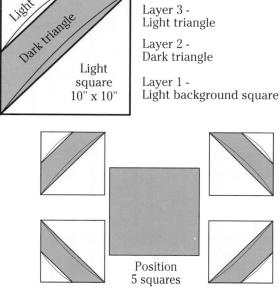

Layer 3 -
Light triangle

Layer 2 -
Dark triangle

Layer 1 -
Light background square

Position
5 squares

BLOCK 10 - RINGS OF SATURN

    Cut 4 Light print-A background squares, each 10" x 10".
    Cut 1 Dark print-B center 'C' square 14" x 14".

Triangles:
    Cut 4 Dark print-B squares for large triangles, each 10" x 10".
        Fold all 4 squares in half diagonally to form triangles. Press.
    Cut 4 Light print-A squares for small triangles, each 5" x 5".
        Fold all 4 squares in half diagonally to form triangles. Press.
    Position a large triangle on each of the 4 Light background squares.
    Position a small triangle on each of the same 4 squares.
        Secure the edges of each triangle to the background square with a ⅛" seam.
        Refer to the Option 2 section of the 10-Minute Block instructions on page 13.
        Roll the bias edge in the shape of a curve and topstitch as in Option 2.

Rings of Saturn Block:
    Position 5 squares as shown.
    Sew the 4 background blocks with the Dark center square following the
        10-Minute method on pages 10 - 13.
    Refer to the Option 2 section of the 10-Minute Block instructions on page 13.
        Roll the bias edge in the shape of a curve and topstitch as in Option 2.

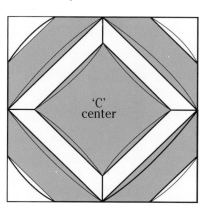

Rings of Saturn

'C' center

Light square
10" x 10"
Cut 1

Light squares
10½" x 10½"
Cut 2

Dark squares
10½" x 10½"
Cut 2

Light/Dark
Half-square
triangles
(see page 18)
Make 4

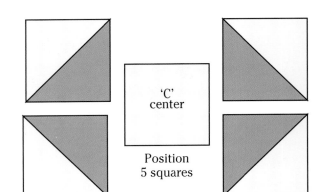

'C' center

Position
5 squares

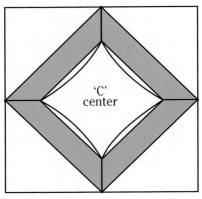

'C' center

Kaleidoscope

BLOCK 11 - KALEIDOSCOPE

Cut 1 Light print-C center 'C' square 10" x 10".
Half-Square Triangles:
Cut 2 Light print-A squares, each 10½" x 10½" .
Cut 2 Dark print-B squares, each 10½" x 10½" .
Make 4 Light/Dark half-square triangles (see page 18).
Center and trim each to 10" x 10". Press.
Kaleidoscope Block:
Arrange the background squares as shown.
Sew the 4 background blocks with the Light center 'C' square
    following the 10-Minute method on pages 10 - 13.
Refer to the Option 2 section of the 10-Minute Block instructions on page 13.
    Roll the bias edge in the shape of a curve and topstitch as in Option 2.

Light squares
10" x 10"
Cut 4

'C' center

Dark square
14" x 14" - Cut 1

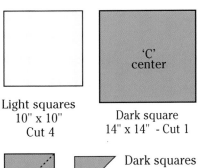

Dark squares
7" x 7"
Cut 4

Fold each Dark square on the
diagonal to form triangles

Dark triangle

Light square
10" x 10"

Position a triangle
on each Light
background square
Make 4

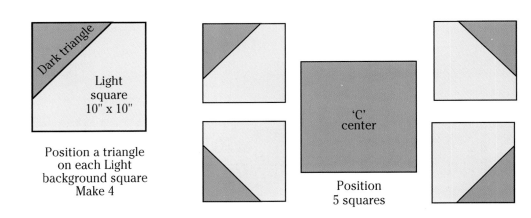

'C' center

Position
5 squares

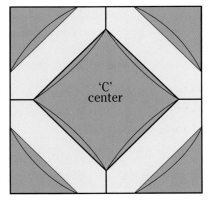

'C' center

Opulence

BLOCK 12 - OPULENCE

Cut 4 Light print-A background squares, each 10" x 10".
Cut 1 Dark print-B center 'C' square 14" x 14".
Triangles:
Cut 4 Dark print-B squares, each 7" x 7".
    Fold all 4 squares in half diagonally to form triangles. Press.
Position a triangle on each of the 4 Light background squares as shown.
    Secure the edges of each triangle to the background square with a ⅛" seam.
    Refer to the Option 2 section of the 10-Minute Block instructions on page 13.
    Roll the bias edge in the shape of a curve and topstitch as in Option 2.
Opulence Block:
Arrange the 4 background squares as shown.
Sew the 4 background blocks with the Dark center square following the
    10-Minute method on pages 10 - 13.
Refer to the Option 2 section of the 10-Minute Block instructions on page 13.
    Roll the bias edge in the shape of a curve and topstitch as in Option 2.

Assembly for Sampler Quilt

photos are on pages 30 - 31

FINISHED SIZE: 77" x 98"

OPTIONAL SETTINGS
Sew the quilt together with 12 different blocks as shown in the diagram
OR
Make 12 blocks from the same pattern and sew these together.

SASHING STRIPS & CORNERSTONES:
    Cut 31 strips of Light print-C for sashing, each $2\frac{1}{2}$" x $19\frac{1}{2}$".
    Cut 20 squares of Dark print-D for cornerstones, each $2\frac{1}{2}$" x $2\frac{1}{2}$".
    Assemble Rows: Sew a sashing strip - block - sashing strip -
        block - sashing strip - block - sashing strip. Press. Make 4 rows.
    Assemble Horizontal Sashing Strips: Sew a cornerstone - sashing strip -
        cornerstone - sashing strip - cornerstone - sashing strip -
        cornerstone. Press. Make 5.

Sampler Quilt Assembly Diagram

BORDER #1:
    Cut $1\frac{1}{2}$" strips across the width of fabric
        and sew together end to end.
    Cut 2 strips $1\frac{1}{2}$" x $86\frac{1}{2}$" for sides.
    Cut 2 strips $1\frac{1}{2}$" x $67\frac{1}{2}$" for the top and
        bottom.
    Sew side borders to the quilt. Press.
    Sew top and bottom borders to the quilt.
        Press.

BORDER #2:
Cut strips $5\frac{1}{2}$" wide parallel to the selvage to
        eliminate piecing.
    Cut 2 strips $5\frac{1}{2}$" x $88\frac{1}{2}$" for sides.
    Cut 2 strips $5\frac{1}{2}$" x $77\frac{1}{2}$" for top and bottom.
    Sew side borders to the quilt. Press.
    Sew top and bottom borders to the quilt.
        Press.

FINISHING:
Quilting: See Basic Instructions.
Binding: Cut strips $2\frac{1}{2}$" wide.
        Sew together end to end to equal 360".
        See Binding Instructions.

Block 1 Four Patch	**Block 2** Framed Window	**Block 3** Hour Glass
Block 4 Starburst	**Block 5** Friendship Star	**Block 6** Sparkle
Block 7 Whirligig	**Block 8** Orange Peel	**Block 9** Sunshine & Shadows
Block 10 Rings of Saturn	**Block 11** Kaleidoscope	**Block 12** Opulence

ASSEMBLY:
    Arrange the blocks and horizontal sashing strips on a work surface.
        You will have 4 rows of 3 blocks each.
    Sew the rows together with a horizontal sashing between the rows. Press.
    Sew a horizontal sashing strip at the top and bottom of the quilt. Press.

Garden Delights

photos are on pages 32 - 33

FINISHED SIZE: 48" x 67"

YARDAGE:

We used fabric from Moda's 'Hoopla' collection
or use the fabric colors of your choice.

Center squares	Purchase ⅝ yard of Dark print
Background squares	Purchase 1¾ yards of Medium stripe
Border #1	Purchase ¼ yard of Dark print
Border #2 & Binding	Purchase 1¾ yards of Medium print
Backing	Purchase 2⅞ yards
Batting	Purchase 56" x 75"

Sewing machine, needle, thread

1. CUT THE 'C' CENTER SQUARES:
Cut 6 Dark print squares, each 14" x 14".

2. CUT SQUARES FOR STRIPED BACKGROUND:
Cut 24 Medium striped background squares, each 10" x 10".

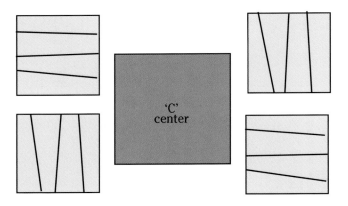

3. 10-MINUTE BLOCKS:
Match a Dark print center with each group of 4 squares.
Refer to the block diagram and note the direction of the stripes in each background square.
Sew the 4 background blocks with the Dark center square following the 10-Minute Block method on pages 10 - 13.
Refer to the Option 2 section of the 10-Minute Block instructions on page 13. Roll the bias edge in the shape of a curve and topstitch as in Option 2.

Large Block - Make 6

4. ASSEMBLY:
Arrange 6 large blocks on a work surface.
Sew 3 rows of 2 blocks each. Press.
Sew the rows together. Press.

5. BORDER #1:
Cut five 1½" strips across the width of fabric and sew together end to end.
Cut 2 strips for the sides, each 1½" x 57½".
Cut 2 strips for the top and bottom, each 1½" x 40½".
Sew side borders to the quilt. Press.
Sew top and bottom borders to the quilt. Press.

Garden Delights Quilt Assembly Diagram

6. BORDER #2:
Cut strips 4½" wide parallel to the selvage to eliminate piecing.
Cut 2 strips for the sides, each 4½" x 59½".
Cut 2 strips for the top and bottom, each 4½" x 48½".
Sew side borders to the quilt. Press.
Sew top and bottom borders to the quilt. Press.

7. FINISHING:
Quilting: See Basic Instructions.
Binding: Cut strips 2½" wide.
Sew together end to end to equal 240".
See Binding Instructions.

Pom Pom de Paris

photos are on pages 34 - 35

FINISHED SIZE: 50" x 68"

YARDAGE:
We used Moda's 'Pom Pom de Paris' collection by French General
    or use the fabric colors of your choice.
Purchase 1 Layer Cake collection OR purchase yardage.

Background squares	Purchase $5/8$ yard of Light prints - color A
Background squares	Purchase $5/8$ yard of Light prints - color B
Background squares	Purchase $5/8$ yard of Light prints - color C
Center squares	Purchase $1/2$ yard of Dark prints
Border #1	Purchase $3/8$ yard of a Dark print-D

    OR purchase $1^2/3$ yard if you want striped fabric in the border

Border #2 & Binding	Purchase $1^2/3$ yards of Dark print-E
Backing	Purchase 3 yards
Batting	Purchase 58" x 76"

Sewing machine, needle, thread

Note: We used assorted prints in each colorway for this
quilt. You can choose to make this quilt in assorted prints
from your stash or make the blocks from matching prints.

1. CUT THE CENTER SQUARES:
    Cut 24 Dark print squares for the centers, each 5" x 5".

2. CUT SQUARES FOR THE BLOCKS:
    Cut 32 Light print A squares for backgrounds, each 5" x 5".
    Cut 32 Light print B squares for backgrounds, each 5" x 5".
    Cut 32 Light print C squares for backgrounds, each 5" x 5".

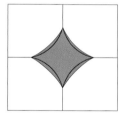

Make 8 of color A

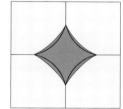

Make 8 of color B

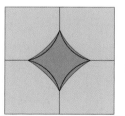

Make 8 of color C

3. 10-MINUTE BLOCKS:
    Group Light background squares into sets of 4 per color.
    Match a Dark center with each group of 4 squares.

    Sew the 4 background blocks with the Dark center
        square following the 10-Minute Block method on
        pages 10 - 13.
    Refer to the Option 2 section of the 10-Minute Block
        instructions on page 13. Roll the bias edge in the
        shape of a curve and topstitch as in Option 2.

    Make 24 blocks - 8 each in color A, color B and color C.

Pom Pom de Paris Quilt Assembly Diagram

4. ASSEMBLY:
    Arrange the blocks on a work surface.
    Sew 6 rows of 4 blocks each. Press.
    Sew the rows together. Press.

5. BORDER #1:
Cut $2^1/2$" strips across the width of fabric and sew together
        end to end.
    Cut 2 strips $2^1/2$" x $54^1/2$" for sides.
    Cut 2 strips $2^1/2$" x $40^1/2$" for the top and bottom.
    Sew side borders to the quilt. Press.
    Sew top and bottom borders to the quilt. Press.

Note: For a 1-way border fabric (ours has vertical
        stripes), cut 2 side strips $2^1/2$" x $54^1/2$" parallel
        to the selvage. To maintain the 1-way design,
        cut 2 strips $2^1/2$" x $40^1/2$" across the width of the
        fabric for the top and bottom.
    Sew side borders to the quilt. Press.
    Sew top and bottom borders to the quilt. Press.

6. BORDER #2:
Cut strips $5^1/2$" wide parallel to the selvage to eliminate piecing.
    Cut 2 strips $5^1/2$" x $58^1/2$" for sides.
    Cut 2 strips $5^1/2$" x $50^1/2$" for top and bottom.
    Sew side borders to the quilt. Press.
    Sew top and bottom borders to the quilt. Press.

7. FINISHING:
Quilting: See Basic Instructions.
Binding: Cut strips $2^1/2$" wide.
        Sew together end to end to equal 246".
        See Binding Instructions.

Large Sampler Quilt

pieced by Donna Arends Hansen
quilted by Sue Needle

Variety is the spice of life. Spice up your quilting with a great sampler. When every block is different, you never get bored. For busy sewers, this quilt is a fun block-of-the-month project, especially if you only have an hour to sew. Speedy techniques make the blocks go together easily.

instructions on pages 21 - 27

Garden Delights

pieced by Edna Summers
quilted by Sue Needle

Soft summer breezes whisper over the garden pond, rippling the surface upon which lotus flowers or lily pads repose. Garden Delights uses the stripes to invoke a soothing sense of water while the bright flowered prints unify the theme. Everyone who gardens or wishes they did will enjoy this quilt. Save the warmth and capture the joy of a sunny day all year round with this happy design.

instructions are on page 28

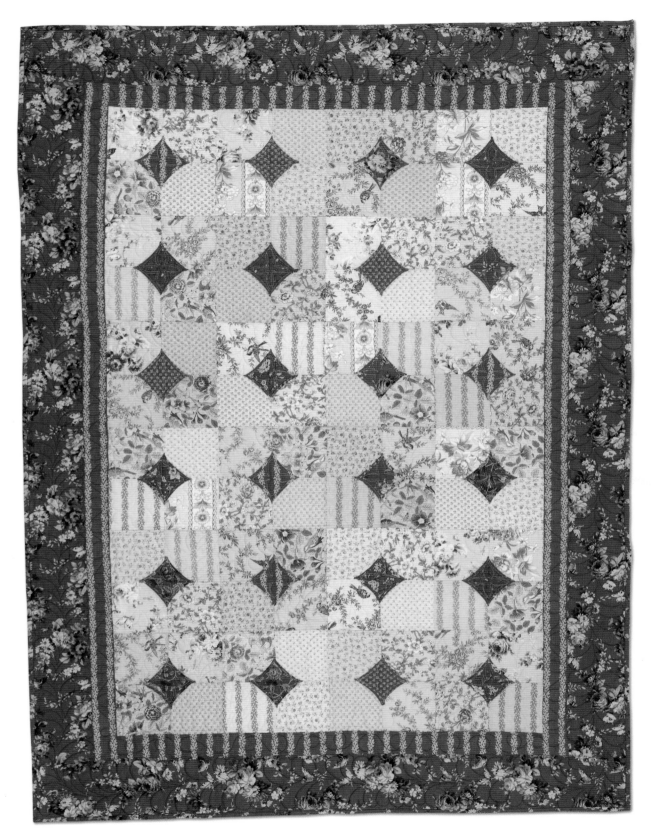

SUPPLIERS

Most quilt and fabric stores carry an excellent assortment of supplies. If you need something special, ask your local store to contact the following companies.

**COTTON FABRICS,
JELLY ROLLS and LAYER CAKES
Moda Fabrics - www.unitednotions.com**

**LONGARM QUILTING BY
Julie Lawson, 817-428-5929
Sue Needle, 817-589-1168**

MANY THANKS to my staff for their cheerful help and wonderful ideas!

Kathy Mason • Janet Long • Donna M.J. Kinsey
David & Donna Thomason